REAL HEROES

STORIES ABOUT
SURVIVING
DRUG ADDICTION

Paul Mason

W
FRANKLIN WATTS
LONDON•SYDNEY

First published in 2010 by Franklin Watts

Copyright © 2010 Arcturus Publishing Limited

Franklin Watts
338 Euston Road
London NW1 3BH

Franklin Watts Australia
Level 17/207 Kent Street, Sydney, NSW 2000

Produced by Arcturus Publishing Limited,
26/27 Bickels Yard, 151–153 Bermondsey Street, London SE1 3HA

The right of Paul Mason to be identified as the author of this work has been asserted by him in accordance with the Copyright, Designs and Patents Act 1988.

Series concept: Alex Woolf
Editor and picture research: Alex Woolf
Designer: Ian Winton

Picture Credits
Corbis: cover (Bob Thomas), 6 (Barbara Walton/epa), 7 (Michael Reynolds/epa), 8 (Ed Kash), 12 (DEA - digital version copyright/Science Faction), 14–15 (Lawrence Manning), 22 (Brenda Ann Kenneally), 27 (Mika), 30 (Hugh Patrick Brown/Sygma), 31 (Scott Houston), 34 (Adrianna Williams), 38 (Chuck Savage), 39 (Darren Kemper/Crush), 42 (Bruno Fert).
Getty Images: 13 (AFP), 17 (Carlos de Andres/Hulton Archive), 21 (Scott Peterson), 23 (Steven L Raymer/National Geographic), 24 (Choo Youn-Kong/AFP), 27 (Sam Panthak/AFP), 35 (Chris Hondros), 36–37 (Jonathan Torgovnik), 43 (Jose Jimenez/Primera Hora).
Shutterstock: 9 (Monkey Business Images), 11 (Jaime Gonzalez), 16 (Klaus-Peter Adler), 19 (Aleksandr Frolov), 20 (Monkey Business Images), 25 (photobank.kiev.ua), 32–33 (Monkey Business Images), 40–41 (ejwhite).

Cover picture: A young drug addict sits on the floor in a public toilet.

Every attempt has been made to clear copyright. Should there be any inadvertent omission, please apply to the publisher for rectification.

A CIP catalogue record for this book is available from the British Library.

Dewey Decimal Classification Number: 362.2'93'0922

ISBN 978 1 4451 0071 5

Printed in China

Franklin Watts is a division of Hachette Children's Books, an Hachette UK company.
www.hachette.co.uk

SL001048EN

Contents

Introduction

What are drugs? Drugs are substances that, when taken into the body, change the way it works. Some drugs change the chemical balance of the brain. For example, they may trigger the release of the chemical dopamine, which leads to feelings of happiness. Some drugs affect the functioning of the body, for example by speeding up a person's heartbeat. Some drugs affect both the mind and the body.

Using drugs

Drugs are often used for medical purposes. For example, ephedrine is a decongestant drug used in today's cold cures. People also use drugs for pleasure. Among the most popular pleasure drugs are alcohol and tobacco. Both of these are legal in many countries, but other pleasure drugs are illegal. These are often called street drugs. Ephedrine, for example, has a pleasure-drug use. It can be used to make another drug, called methamphetamine, which produces feelings of intense pleasure.

Different types of drug

Drugs can be divided into three main categories, based on their effects: stimulants, depressants and psychoactive drugs.

- stimulants speed up the body's functions. They make your heart beat faster, increase your blood pressure and make you feel more alert and lively. Popular stimulants include cocaine, amphetamines, caffeine (in coffee and tea) and nicotine (in cigarettes).
- depressants slow down the body's functions. They slow down your heart rate, you breathe more slowly and you feel more relaxed. Your speech can become slurred and you can lose coordination. Popular depressants include alcohol, GHB, heroin and sleeping pills.
- Psychoactive drugs affect the way people see, hear

◀ **The white powder is heroin and the red pills are metamphetamines. They have been seized by police in Thailand in a crackdown on illegal drugs. Part of Thailand called the Golden Triangle is famous for growing opium, from which heroin is made.**

► This woman in China is a heroin addict, and also has HIV/AIDS. This deadly disease is more common among heroin addicts than other people, because they share needles to inject the drug. The used needle carries the disease from one addict to the next.

and feel. They may result in people sensing things that are not, in fact, there. Popular psychoactive drugs include LSD, MDMA (which is found in ecstasy) and ketamine.

Some drugs combine more than one of these: cannabis, for example, is both a depressant and a psychoactive drug. Ecstasy is a psychoactive drug, but is often cut, or mixed in, with the stimulant speed.

Drug addiction

People who take drugs regularly risk becoming addicted – they come to depend on the drug so strongly that they believe they cannot live without it. People who start taking drugs do not plan to become addicts. But their need for drugs grows ever more powerful until it is the most important thing in their lives. Everything else – family, friends and work – comes second to their need for drugs.

Top ten most dangerous drugs

In 2007, a British study tried to work out which ten drugs were the most dangerous. The study used three measures for working out how dangerous a drug was: the harm it did to the user, its addictiveness and its impact on society. This was their conclusion (1 being the most dangerous and 10 being the least):

1. Heroin
2. Cocaine
3. Barbiturates
4. Street methadone
5. Alcohol
6. Ketamine
7. Benzodiazepine
8. Amphetamine
9. Tobacco
10. Buprenorphine

Cannabis came in at 11, LSD at 14 and ecstasy at 18.

Source: *The Lancet*, March 2007

▶ **This young woman in San Francisco, USA, is suffering from withdrawal, the physical effects of trying to stop taking drugs. Her joints are aching and she feels feverish, and she thinks that only drugs will make her feel well again.**

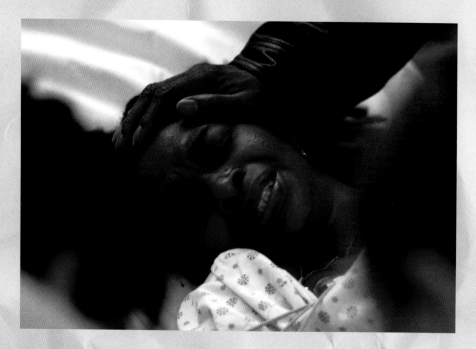

Drug addiction and health

Drug addiction can affect the user's health in different ways, depending on the drug:

• Some drugs – ketamine, LSD and skunk cannabis, for example – have been associated with mental illnesses.

• Alcohol can cause liver disease, heart problems, cancer and brain damage.

• Many drugs carry a risk of overdose. Overdose is when the drug's effect is so strong that the body shuts down, causing severe illness or death.

• Drugs that are injected, such as heroin, carry the risk of infection by deadly diseases such as HIV and hepatitis B. This is because the users sometimes share needles, and the disease is passed from one person to the next in the needle.

• Drugs often cause people to lose their inhibitions and act in ways they would not normally consider. This can include violence or reckless sexual behaviour (making drug takers more likely to fall prey to sexually transmitted diseases).

Drugs and families

Drug addiction affects the families of addicts as well as the addicts themselves. As the stories in this book show, drug addicts sometimes steal from their parents, neglect their children or abuse their husband or wife because of their need for drugs.

The cost of drugs

Drugs are expensive, and few addicts have enough money of their own to pay for the drugs they need. Many become involved in crime, including robbery, burglary, shoplifting and prostitution, as a way of paying for their drugs.

Drugs cost money in other ways, too. Governments spend huge sums each year on law enforcement, the justice system and prisons to deal with drug-related crime.

The treatments addicts need cost health services huge sums of money each year. All of this must be paid for by taxes.

Escaping drug addiction

Given the harm they do to other people and society in general, it is tempting to think that drug addicts deserve no sympathy. But no one who tries a drug for the first time is planning to become an addict. Those who do become addicted to drugs are trapped in a world where the drug takes over their lives. Escaping takes hard work and dedication, and many addicts fail.

This book tells the stories of young people directly affected by drug addiction, the difficulties they have encountered and how they have survived. The stories are all true, but people's names and some aspects of their identity have been changed.

A deadly habit

• Worldwide, 20–24 million people are addicted to illegal drugs.

• Roughly 200,000 people die each year as a result of taking illegal drugs.

• Nearly two million die as a result of alcohol abuse.

• Five million die as a result of smoking cigarettes.

Source: United Nations World Drug Report, 2009

▼ **The man in the car is buying street drugs in a small plastic bag. Until he tries them, he cannot be sure what the bag contains or what other substances the drugs have been mixed with.**

Bill's Story

Until the middle of high school, Bill was a normal boy, with better-than-average grades. He enjoyed football and basketball and hanging out with his childhood friends. But then things began to change. Bill's mum noticed that his grades were slipping, and he was no longer interested in sport. Finally, an overheard telephone conversation revealed the truth: Bill was into drugs. It was the start of a long fight to get well again.

Bill clearly remembers the first time he took drugs. He was 12 years old and Steve, one of the cool kids from school, invited him over to his house to smoke cannabis. Scared of taking drugs, but more scared of being seen as uncool, Bill agreed to go. After his first joint (cigarette containing cannabis), he was hooked. Soon, he was going over to his new friend's house every night to smoke cannabis. Then he and Steve started smoking in the mornings before school, and during lunch break as well. A small bag of cannabis cost about five dollars – the same as a cafeteria lunch.

In senior high school, Bill began to use a much wider variety of drugs. He had started going to raves, and the depressant effects of cannabis didn't match the music they played there. Some of the other dancers were taking ecstasy pills, and Bill started doing the same. He was beginning to use different drugs to match whatever situation he found himself in: cannabis when he wanted to relax, ecstasy when he wanted to feel lively. Soon Bill began to use other drugs as well. Cocaine made him feel confident; LSD made him feel very imaginative; ketamine gave him tremendous energy. Finally, Bill got hooked on methamphetamine, a drug he now says made him feel 'completely invincible'.

The effects of smoking cannabis

Smoking cannabis regularly over a long period can have significant effects on your mental health. Cannabis use has been linked to:

- problems with memory

- paranoia (feeling that other people are out to get you, or that something bad is about to happen)

- hallucinations and delusions (seeing or imagining things that don't exist)

- mental illnesses, especially schizophrenia

The effects of cannabis use may be worse among smokers of 'skunk' cannabis, which can have as much as three times the amount of active ingredient.

▶ **Rolling a cigarette containing a mixture of cannabis and tobacco. Many people's first experience of illegal drugs is when they smoke cannabis. Evidence suggests that cannabis can be harmful to people's mental health.**

On Friday, Saturday and Sunday nights, after dancing all night at rave clubs and taking all kinds of drugs, Bill and his friends would climb back into the car and head home. Bill remembers that drivers would regularly fall asleep at the wheel, only to be woken up by the horns of other motorists.

All the while, Bill was able to hide his drug addiction from his mother by claiming he was going camping or staying with a friend. But the day was soon coming when all that would change.

Bill's world finally began to go to pieces when he got hooked on methamphetamine. 'Meth' is a psychostimulant, which gives users a feeling of intense pleasure. But the 'comedown' as the drug leaves their system can be very unpleasant. Users feel depressed and anxious and crave drugs – particularly more meth. In comparison with the meth high, events that people would normally find pleasurable begin to seem dull and uninteresting.

Methamphetamine

Methamphetamine is a highly addictive drug. There are several different names for methamphetamine, including meth, crank, ice and crystal. One sign that someone is using the drug is 'meth mouth': rotten teeth that eventually fall out. Users very quickly develop a physical and psychological reliance on the drug, and are only able to feel happy when taking it.

Bill had always been careful not to take drugs at home. But his meth addiction made him much less cautious. His mum walked into his room as he was in the process of sniffing speed, a stimulant, before heading off to his Saturday job. Bill barged past her and left, but when he got home that night his mum and dad were waiting for him. They put Bill into a

▼ **Methamphetamine powder in a foil wrapper. Taking 'meth' leads the brain to release dopamine, causing tremendous happiness. Once the drug wears off, the happiness is replaced by a feeling of emptiness, which only more meth can end.**

▲ **A British man is arrested in Bali, Indonesia, after being caught with methamphetamine. Like many countries, Indonesia has strict punishments for people found guilty of selling drugs.**

rehab (rehabilitation) centre, where he spent the next three weeks. But when he got out, Bill quickly slid back into his old ways. His mum knew what he was up to, but couldn't find a way of stopping him.

Bill had been stealing to pay for drugs for years, but had never been caught. When the police did finally catch up with him, it was for a traffic offence. The officer searched Bill's car and discovered all kinds of drug material: a glass pipe for smoking drugs, some speed, a small mirror and credit card for chopping drugs up fine enough to sniff, and 'baggies' – small, clear plastic bags for keeping drugs in. Bill was handcuffed and put in the back of the police car, arrested and charged. Finally, in the cells at the police station, the reality of the situation hit Bill. It wasn't a game: he could be going to jail.

Bill's mum managed to get him released on bail the next day. He immediately asked her to help him get treatment for his addiction. By the end of the week he had signed up for a six-month course of drug counselling. Since the course ended Bill has not taken any kind of drug, even legal drugs such as alcohol. He now has a job, a girlfriend and hope for a brighter future. As Bill admits, 'I don't really want to think about how many brain cells I've lost – a lot. I wish I'd never smoked that first joint. But now my life has improved a hundred per cent.'

Juanita's Story

Juanita lives in Florida, USA. Soon after getting married, she had a son called Mike and a daughter named Sue. Mike got into drugs and eventually died of a heroin overdose. His death has had a terrible effect on his family, who are all still learning to live with what happened.

Mike first tried drugs when he was a teenager. He soon began behaving differently. He would be tired and irritable and could not get up in the morning. After a night out with his friends he would spend the whole day in bed. Juanita remembered her own teenage

Clubbing drugs

Clubbers have been known to use a range of different drugs, including ecstasy, GHB and ketamine. Ecstasy is a stimulant, which speeds your heart rate and causes mood changes. It is linked with depression, mood swings and lethargy, and strains the heart, liver and kidneys. GHB gives a feeling of relaxation when taken in small doses. In larger doses it causes sickness, numbness in the arms and legs, and muscle spasms. GHB has been used as a date rape drug. Ketamine is a psychoactive and anaesthetic drug that affects people in wildly different ways. It has been linked to impaired memory and schizophrenia.

years, going out dancing, and thought Mike was doing the same thing. Mike said she was right: he liked to dance, drink beer and sometimes smoke cannabis. In fact, Mike had become a hardcore ecstasy user.

Juanita now knows that she missed the clues that might have told her what was happening to Mike. For example, he often had sneezes and a runny nose. Mike would complain of backache. Juanita thought he was getting flu or a heavy cold. In fact he was suffering from something known as dope sick – one of the symptoms of heavy drug use.

Mike was going out to rave clubs and taking ecstasy. The last time his mother saw him, his brain had been so badly affected by drug use that, she says, 'He could not even follow a simple conversation'. Not long afterwards Juanita got the news that Mike had died of a heroin overdose. He was 26. Tests proved that he had been a heavy ecstasy user for years.

Mike's death caused terrible pain to his family. He left behind a mother, sister, ex-wife and son, all of whose lives were damaged by his addiction and death. Juanita decided she wanted to do something to stop other families from suffering the same experience. She now works as a drug counsellor for young people and their families, educating them about the dangerous effects of drug use.

◀ **Since it began in the 1980s, the rave scene has been associated with drugs such as ecstasy. But drugs, high temperatures inside clubs, alcohol and dancing all night make a dangerous combination, and many deaths have resulted.**

Anders' Story

Anders lives in Denmark. He started taking drugs because he felt they might make him more successful at school and more entertaining in social situations. Soon he became an addict, and it took Anders ten years to kick his drugs habit and start to live a normal life. Today, though, he uses his terrible experiences to help other people avoid making the same mistakes he did.

Throughout his childhood Anders thought his parents were not interested in him. As he grew older, he developed a very negative attitude. He was angry that his life was not going better, jealous of people who seemed more successful than him and depressed at the thought that things would never improve. Most of all he felt constantly afraid – of what, he was not sure.

Things changed for Anders when he discovered alcohol and drugs. Unfortunately, they did not change for the better. At first, when Anders was afraid, alcohol took away his fear. When he was angry, smoking cannabis calmed him down. Soon he began using a wide variety of drugs to change his moods. It was not long before Anders could no longer tell what he was really feeling. If he was paranoid, was he *really* paranoid, or was it the after-effects of smoking cannabis? When he felt invincible, was he *really* confident, or was it because he had been sniffing cocaine? Anders' negative feelings returned, stronger than ever.

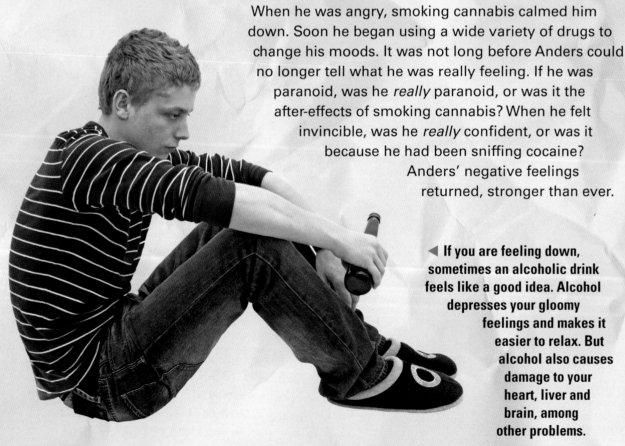

◀ If you are feeling down, sometimes an alcoholic drink feels like a good idea. Alcohol depresses your gloomy feelings and makes it easier to relax. But alcohol also causes damage to your heart, liver and brain, among other problems.

▲ People trying to beat their drug addiction attend a therapy session. Many addicts find that hearing about other people's battles with drugs, and speaking about their own, helps them to beat their addiction.

After ten years as an addict, Anders realized that if he did not stop taking drugs, they would kill him. As he says now, 'I could not imagine life without drugs – but I found it even harder to imagine being dead!' He began to go to group counselling sessions. He met with other addicts at Alcoholics Anonymous and Narcotics Anonymous. Anders' counsellor helped him see that drugs were making his problems worse, not better.

Inspired by the example of his counsellor, Anders decided to become one himself. As soon as he had been drug-free for a year, he began training to help other people get themselves off drugs and alcohol. He now works with drug addicts and alcoholics in the city of Odense. Anders says his recovery from addiction has been tough, but he now gets a great reward from helping others start the same journey to a drug-free life.

Group therapy

Group therapy is one of the most common ways of helping people get themselves off drugs and stay off drugs. A counsellor leads the group: his or her role is to get people talking about their actions. Together, the group will discuss things such as:

- why members started taking drugs
- the actions their drug addiction caused them to take
- how drug addiction has affected their lives and the lives of people around them
- the challenges they face in trying to stay off drugs

Carmel's Story

Most drug addicts start their drug-taking careers with alcohol. Some then move on to different kinds of drug, such as cannabis or ecstasy. Others, like Carmel, stick with alcohol. Carmel's story shows that even though it is a legal drug, alcohol can be just as hard to beat as illegal ones.

Carmel lives in Melbourne, Australia. She first tasted alcohol at the age of 12 and immediately enjoyed the feeling of confidence and relaxation it gave her. At 16 she left school and started work, and the extra money she earned made it possible for her to start drinking more. Every night she went into a bar for a drink, or took alcohol home. At 25 Carmel got a job as a barmaid. She began drinking increasing quantities. Carmel became an alcohol addict, or alcoholic.

Carmel was drinking her way through huge amounts of money. Her aunt died and left her an inheritance of 20,000 Australian dollars. Carmel managed to spend all of it on alcohol in just 6 months. When that money ran out, she started stealing from her employer to fund her drinking.

Alcohol was also costing Carmel her health. She was finally admitted to hospital suffering from delirium tremens, a serious illness caused by alcohol withdrawal. When doctors

The effects of alcohol

Alcohol is a depressant drug and it has an immediate effect on the human body. The effects can be divided into four stages:

1. Alcohol is at first absorbed very quickly. It depresses fears and inhibitions, making people feel happy and confident.

2. If the drinking continues, it begins to affect coordination, making even simple tasks such as walking more difficult. Reactions get slower and speech becomes slurred. Crucially, decision making – including the decision to stop drinking – becomes increasingly difficult.

3. The body recognizes that alcohol is putting it in danger and tries to break it down and expel it through the liver and in urine. But it cannot keep up with the amount of alcohol being drunk, so the effects get worse.

4. If the drinking continues, the body begins to stop working. Heart rate slows, and the brain becomes more likely to drop into a coma. Finally, the central nervous system shuts down, causing death.

▶ **Because alcohol makes people feel less self-conscious, lots of us drink at parties and other social occasions. But drinking too much can mean that we behave in ways that will seem *very* embarrassing once the effects of alcohol have worn off.**

warned her that her heart and liver had already been badly damaged by alcohol, Carmel realized it was time to do something about her drinking.

Carmel began going to meetings of Alcoholics Anonymous. She got counselling and went to meetings with other alcoholics. This helped her to see how alcohol was ruining her life and gave her the determination to beat her alcoholism. Carmel has now been 'dry' – or alcohol-free – for three years.

Adrian's Story

Many people drink small amounts of alcohol, then stop drinking before the drug affects them too strongly. Some, though – like Adrian, from Wellington, New Zealand – seem not to know when to stop drinking. By the time he was 23, Adrian was so addicted to alcohol that it almost ruined his life. He ended up far from home, on the other side of the world, without money or friends. Without the help of his family, Adrian might never have made it back to normal life.

Adrian first started drinking when he was 14. He felt that alcohol relaxed him and made him more confident among other people. He was just an ordinary teenager, neither especially good nor especially bad at anything. He didn't stand out in a crowd – but all that changed when he and his friends discovered alcohol. They began to drink 'fast and furious', as Adrian says. Even among this crowd, Adrian stood out. He became famous for drinking so much that he became unconscious. Sometimes he would come round, be sick, and start drinking again.

Many of Adrian's friends began to get jobs and have girlfriends. They stopped drinking such large amounts of alcohol. Adrian, however, couldn't stop: he had become an alcoholic. Few of his old friends wanted to hang out with him any more. Someone

▶ Not having a drink can lead to name-calling and bullying, so drinking beer with your mates is one way of fitting in. Sometimes this even turns into a competition to see who can get the most drunk.

◀ **This young man is doing carpentry in a workshop near Moscow, Russia. He is part of a scheme in which young drinkers live at the workshop and learn new skills, and at the same time give up alcohol.**

who was busy drinking himself unconscious wasn't very much fun to be around. Adrian decided he needed a new start. He moved to London, England.

When Adrian got to London, he found himself slipping back into his old ways. Most of his friends were fellow New Zealanders living in London. They met up in pubs and spent a lot of their spare time drinking. It wasn't long before Adrian was once again drinking until he passed out. He was drunk so often that every time he phoned home, his speech was slurred and he couldn't concentrate on what was being said.

Adrian's family became so worried about him that they decided he had to come home and get help. His brother flew to the UK. Adrian admitted he had a problem with his drinking, but could not stop. Together, they flew back to New Zealand. Adrian went into rehab. Group therapy sessions allowed Adrian to see a path away from alcohol addiction. Now aged 28, he has been dry for three years.

Long-term effects of alcohol

When it is drunk in large amounts over a long period of time, alcohol begins to have very serious effects on the human body. Some of these are reversible if the person stops drinking; others cannot be undone.

- Heart and liver damage are common among alcohol abusers.

- Dementia and mental health problems can be caused by heavy alcohol consumption.

- Cancer, strokes, panic attacks, stomach and digestive problems, and impotence can all be caused by alcohol.

Tracey's Story

Tracey lives in Nottingham, England. Because neither of her parents could look after her, Tracey was brought up in care. She lived in a variety of foster families and children's homes. Tracey started taking drugs before she was even a teenager. Later, her own children were taken away to live elsewhere because she could not look after them. This gave Tracey the determination to get herself off drugs and get her children back.

Tracey first started taking drugs when she was 11 years old. She began with alcohol, offered to her by some older children. It was cheap cider, which she drank from a plastic bottle. Before long Tracey was drinking regularly. Next she began smoking cannabis, and then heroin. Within a few years – before she had even finished school – Tracey was a heroin addict.

Tracey had her first baby when she was 15. The baby was soon taken away from her, to be looked after by the authorities. Tracey's drug addiction, combined with her age, made it impossible for her to look after her child. She had more children, and each was soon taken away to live elsewhere. When her youngest baby was born, it was taken away straight from the hospital. Tracey decided she had to kick her drug addiction so she could get her daughter back.

She went to stay at a residential centre run by a local charity. The centre's aim was to help young people with children give up drugs. It also taught them how to look after their children properly. Tracey had no idea how to do this because she had never had a chance to learn it from her own mother or

▲ This woman is smoking crack cocaine – a very pure form of the drug – while her daughter sleeps. Eight of her children have already been taken into care because she cannot look after them properly.

Children in care

Drug addicts who have children run the risk that their kids will be taken away from them. This is because being a drug addict makes it very difficult to look after your children properly.

- Money that should be spent on clothes, food or things for school may instead be spent on drugs.

- Someone under the influence of drugs may fail to watch out for a child's safety.

- Drug addicts may be more focused on taking drugs than on preparing their children's meals and making sure they do their homework or go to bed on time.

- Drug addicts may pass their own drug-taking habits onto their children.

father. At first she found all the rules at the centre difficult to stick to: rules about cleaning, timekeeping and behaviour. But she began to make progress. Eventually she left the centre, having given up drugs.

Today, Tracey lives in a small house with her daughter. Her other children do not live there, but they come and stay regularly. 'It feels like we're a family,' she says. 'I'm just grateful for all the help I got when I was trying to give up drugs.'

▼ These mothers in Los Angeles, USA, are all heroin addicts. They are living in a home where they can stop taking drugs and begin to build a new life for themselves and their children.

Sarah's Story

Drug addiction does not only affect the addicts themselves. It also affects their families. When Michelle became addicted to heroin, she was no longer able to look after her child, Tyler. He needed to live with someone who would make sure he was fed, clothed and kept safe. He went to stay with Michelle's mother, Sarah.

Michelle was introduced to heroin by a boyfriend, who was addicted to the drug. At first she only took heroin once in a while, but as time went by she began injecting the drug more and more often. Whatever Sarah said, she could not persuade Michelle to stop taking heroin.

Michelle's young son Tyler began to be affected by his mother's drug taking. Sarah noticed that he was missing school because his mother could not get out of bed to take him there. Sometimes Michelle took heroin and forgot to collect Tyler from school. Then she began to leave Tyler on his own at weekends while she went out to get drugs. Sarah stepped in and suggested that Tyler come and live with her.

▶ **This young Indonesian woman first became a heroin addict when she was 21. Since then she has lost her husband, son and job – but still she has not managed to beat her addiction.**

◀ This young boy is picking wild flowers with his grandmother. The children of drug addicts regularly end up being looked after by their grandparents.

Today, Tyler only misses school when he is ill. He has his own room, clean clothes to wear and eats plenty of food. He misses living with his mum, but is doing well at school and loves his grandmother.

Michelle is not doing so well. She was recently taken into hospital with blood clots on her heart, caused by her drug use. Sarah hoped Michelle would be scared into giving up drugs and getting help with her addiction, but this hasn't happened. Instead, Michelle often disappears for weeks on end. No one is sure where she is, and Tyler never knows when, or even if, he will see his mum again.

Heroin

Heroin is a drug made from the opium poppy. It has existed for more than a hundred years and is sometimes used by doctors as a painkiller. Heroin is also one of the most popular illegal drugs in the world. It is usually injected into the user's veins, but heroin can also be smoked or sniffed. As the drug hits the brain, users get a 'rush' — a feeling of intense excitement, followed by extreme happiness and relaxation. Heroin use can cause various problems:

- The chance of physical addiction is very high.

- Users run the risk of overdosing or being poisoned by chemicals mixed with the drug.

- Users risk being infected with viruses such as HIV while injecting the drug.

- Heroin can cause chronic constipation.

- It can damage the kidneys.

Mike's Story

For drug addicts, getting hold of drugs and using them are the most important things in their lives. Everything else – family, friends and children – comes second. Mike lives in Scunthorpe in the UK. His story shows how drug use can affect the children of drug addicts. But it also shows that it is possible for even the most addicted drug user to give up drugs and become a proper father to his children.

Mike and his partner were both long-term drug addicts. They had got into drugs while they were teenagers and quickly became addicted. Living in housing provided by their local authority, they claimed benefits and stole money to pay for drugs. Later, they had two children, Matty and Jake. Looking back, Mike says he knows how tough the boys must have found it growing up. At any time either their mum or dad was usually absent – in drug treatment centres, psychiatric centres or prison. Even when they were there, the boys' parents were more interested in drugs than their kids.

Mike remembers one example of how he always put drugs first. He was driving somewhere with his kids in the back of the car when he crashed into a parked car. The owners were very kind and invited Mike and the kids into their house for a cup of tea to calm down. Mike's first action was not to check that Matty and Jake were OK – instead he went into the toilet to jack up (inject himself) with drugs.

Mike hit a turning point while he was in a methadone clinic. One day a nurse asked him how his children coped with their dad's drug addiction. Mike says it struck him like a bolt of lightning: he had never even thought about the effect it had had on his kids. He became determined to kick his drugs habit.

It was a long struggle for Mike to give up drugs. Like most addicts, he tried many times before he was successful. As well as going to drug counselling, Mike went on parenting courses to learn how to be a good dad. Once he had removed drugs from his life, he was finally able to put his kids first. Unfortunately, Mike's partner hasn't yet been able to give up drugs. She now only sees her children every few weeks.

Methadone

Methadone is a drug used to help heroin addicts give up drugs. It acts on the same receptors in the brain as opiates such as heroin. Used in the right doses, methadone blocks the feelings of happiness and relaxation that are caused by heroin. Because the addicts no longer get high, methadone makes it easier for them to give up heroin.

▲ **Many drug addicts find it impossible to look after their children properly. Drugs have become the most important thing in their life. They pay little attention to their kids and may not provide them with the food and clothing they need.**

Today Mike is a very different person from the drug addict he was. He works hard at two part-time jobs, cooks for his kids, makes sure their homework gets done and is an all-round good dad. He also spends time teaching parenting skills to other drug addicts.

Janie's Story

Janie lives in Glasgow, UK, a city with a higher than average number of drug addicts. Janie was addicted to heroin. Her addiction made her very ill, threatening the health of her baby. However, she has recently beaten her addiction with the help of methadone.

When Janie was nine, her parents split up and she and her mother moved to a new town. Janie was unhappy about leaving her friends and had frequent arguments with her mum. To escape the bad atmosphere at home, Janie spent time on the streets with other kids who were also unhappy in their home lives. Some of them were into sniffing glue, and Janie joined in. Soon afterwards they began to use heroin instead, and Janie was hooked.

Hepatitis B

Hepatitis B is a disease of the liver. Sometimes it is a short sickness that quickly dies down without causing long-term damage. In about 20 per cent of cases the sickness lasts six months or longer, and may lead to death. Hepatitis B is highly infectious and is caught via the blood or body fluids of an infected person. This makes people who inject drugs and share needles with other drug users especially likely to catch the disease. Hepatitis B can also be passed on during unprotected sex, at childbirth and in a mother's breast milk.

Janie contracted a disease called hepatitis B when she was 25, after sharing a needle with another drug addict. By this time she had had two children. Not long after catching the disease she became pregnant with her third child.

Janie was worried about this because hepatitis B can be passed on to babies at birth, or in the mother's breast milk. Also, the babies of heroin and methadone users are born with an addiction to the drug themselves. Normally, methadone addicts can breastfeed their babies as a way of helping to ease the baby off drugs. However, Janie's hepatitis B made breastfeeding very risky.

Janie was able to work with her doctors to have a healthy baby. When it was born, the doctors took extra precautions to make sure the baby did not get infected with hepatitis B. They gave the baby a vaccine against the disease. It was not long before Janie was able to start breastfeeding her baby.

Spurred on by this positive outcome, Janie asked her health worker to reduce her methadone dosage. Next she managed to stop taking methadone completely, or any other drug. Janie got herself a place on a beauty therapy course and is now working in one of Glasgow's beauty salons. She has been drug-free for three years.

▲ This three-day-old baby is being held by his aunt. They live near Ahmedabad, India. The baby's mother died of hepatitis B after being injected with a used needle.

Amy's Story

Amy lives in Hastings on the south coast of England. She started using drugs at the age of 11. Amy's story is unusual because of how she got into drugs in the first place. She didn't have to worry about her parents discovering that she was developing a drug habit – they already knew. It was her father who gave Amy her first taste of cannabis.

Amy spent her childhood surrounded by drugs. Her father sold drugs from their house, so there were always addicts around. Amy's father enjoyed super-strength beer and skunk cannabis, but many of his friends and customers were heroin addicts. He would let them shoot up (inject themselves) in the bathroom and toilet, then lie around the house until the effect of the drug had worn away.

Amy first tried drugs when she was 11. She sniffed glue, and soon afterwards was given her first cannabis cigarette by her father. By the time she was a teenager, Amy had moved on to smoking crack cocaine. It would be over 20 years before Amy would be able to rid herself of her addiction to crack.

Amy had children of her own when she was quite young. She used the child benefit money, which was meant to pay for the children's clothes and food, to pay for drugs. Amy went on to have six children, and all of them were affected by her addiction. She paid them little attention, and her three youngest children were so badly looked after that the local authorities took them into care.

▶ Tiny containers hold 'rocks' of crack. Behind them is a glass pipe, the kind that many addicts use to smoke the drug.

▶ 'At this shelter there is hope,' says this young drug addict. She has come to a shelter for drug addicts in Tulsa, USA. She hopes it will help her make a better life for herself and her baby daughter.

Many people would say that with a childhood like hers, it was inevitable that Amy would become hooked on drugs. Even so, in her 30s she realized that drugs were ruining her life, and her children's. She undertook drugs counselling. Amy had had counselling before but, as she says, 'This time I was determined it would succeed'. She finally managed to get herself drug-free, but her drug addiction had left a terrible legacy. Her three youngest children have never lived with her, and one of her older children is now a drug user herself.

Drug use and families

In 2009 a UK survey into the ways in which drug use by a parent affects their children discovered the following:

- Some children had tried heroin at 12 or 13 as a result of being offered it by their mother or father.

- By the time they were between 10 and 14, a quarter of the children of drug addicts had tried drugs or alcohol.

- Between 15 and 17 years old, over half of the children had started habitually using drugs or alcohol.

- Many of the children said they had started taking drugs because it was the only way they could feel closer to their parents, who were otherwise not interested in them.

Source: UK Department of Health, reported in the *Guardian*, 14 January 2009

Mika's Story

Today, Mika lives happily in an apartment in St Petersburg, Russia. He has plenty of friends, a wife and a young family. Mika has a job he loves as a tour guide showing visitors the wonderful buildings and art galleries of the city. Not long ago, however, Mika was a very different man. His addictions to alcohol and various drugs had left him physically close to death – and almost suicidal with despair.

Mika's first addiction was to alcohol. As a young man he would go out and binge drink until he was sick. After vomiting, he would carry on drinking more alcohol. Other drugs did not interest Mika. In fact, he disapproved of them. Only once did he try illegal drugs, when his girlfriend took him to a party and gave him an ecstasy pill. Although he enjoyed it, Mika decided not to take ecstasy again. Instead, during a long stay in Spain, Mika spent all his time drinking, often until he was unconscious.

When Mika got back from his holiday, he felt that his life was dull and uninteresting. He remembered enjoying the party, and the pill, his old girlfriend had given him. Mika began to get into the rave scene, going to all-night parties and drinking huge amounts of alcohol. Soon he was mixing alcohol with ecstasy – a very dangerous combination. It wasn't long before Mika was hooked on a combination of alcohol, ecstasy and packet after packet of cigarettes.

Next, Mika started taking amphetamines at raves. Before long he was addicted to those as well. Mika could not imagine life without drugs. He even took drugs in his luggage when he went abroad, risking prison if he was caught.

The abuse Mika was putting his body through started to affect his health. He had to wear a mouth guard at night after taking amphetamines because the drug was causing him to grind his teeth and break them while he was asleep. Next, Mika was admitted to hospital with heart palpitations (an irregular heartbeat). Even after this had happened for the second time, Mika refused any help.

▶ **Drinking alcohol on its own is dangerous: drink enough and it will kill you. Mixing large amounts of alcohol with drugs makes the risks even greater.**

Alcohol and ecstasy

Mixing alcohol and ecstasy is very dangerous and has caused several deaths. The effects of the two drugs combine in a way that can quickly cause the user's body to stop working:

- Ecstasy affects the chemical serotonin inside the body. Serotonin helps control the body's temperature: taking ecstasy causes the temperature to rise.

- Dancing in a hot club — which ecstasy, a stimulant, encourages — causes dehydration, which further increases the body's temperature.

- Drinking alcohol also causes dehydration.

- If dehydration becomes too severe, the liver, brain and heart stop working properly, which can lead to death.

▶ **A drug user's 'kit': cocaine powder, a razor blade for chopping the powder up fine enough to snort, and a rolled-up banknote to use for sucking it into the nose.**

Mika knew he had to do something about the amount of alcohol and drugs he was consuming. He decided that he would deal with the problem himself, simply by deciding to give up. For a short time this worked. Mika became convinced that, having been able to stop taking drugs, he was in control of his addiction. He thought he could start and stop taking drugs whenever necessary. So Mika started taking drugs again. This time, though, he tried cocaine – one of the most addictive drugs available. Mika's life quickly began to fall apart.

School, work and drugs

Almost all drugs affect how people behave at school or at work:

- All drugs affect concentration and judgement and make people behave differently from normal.

- The physical after-effects of drugs, including headaches, tiredness and irritability, can make it harder to study or work.

- Psychoactive drugs such as LSD can have long-term psychological effects, causing users to suffer flashbacks and memory loss.

- Alcohol and cannabis have been associated with memory loss and can cause physical damage to the brain.

Cocaine is expensive, yet Mika took it every day, from the moment he woke up until the time he passed out on the sofa in the evening. This amounted to a very costly habit. But, because of his addiction, Mika earned less and less money. He had become unreliable, failing to turn up for jobs and not concentrating on his work when he did manage to get there.

Soon all his savings were gone, and his credit cards were at their limit. Mika stopped opening his post: he owed so many people money that it was only ever a letter containing a demand for repayment.

Mika finally realized that his addiction was out of control. It seemed impossible to get back to a normal, drug-free life, and he thought about killing himself. In the end, though, he rang his sister. Together they contacted a drug counselling service, and Mika went to meet a counsellor. That was the moment he started to turn his life around.

Today, Mika is drug-free, and has been for four years. He is determined never to go back to drugs. Whenever he gets into a situation where he might once have taken amphetamine, drunk alcohol or snorted cocaine, he goes to a meeting of Narcotics Anonymous. There, Mika is guaranteed to meet other people who have also survived drug addiction and who will know how to encourage him not to go back to his old ways. Mika has a lot to live for: he has a wife, two small children, a nice home and a job he loves. As he says: 'Why would I give all that up now for the misery of drugs?'

▲ The men sitting on the ground are all Afghan heroin addicts. They are at a treatment centre in Pakistan. Between them, Pakistan and Afghanistan are the source of much of the world's heroin.

Tonya's Story

Ayear ago, Tonya's life was going nowhere fast. She had been a drug addict since she was 15. Having started with cannabis, she ended up taking heroin regularly, going out to buy ten-dollar bags on the street corners of Baltimore, USA. Today, though – with the help of her family – Tonya has managed to get herself clean of drugs.

At 13 Tonya had her first experience of cocaine. She loved the feeling of excitement and confidence it gave her and began taking it more and more often. Because cocaine is a

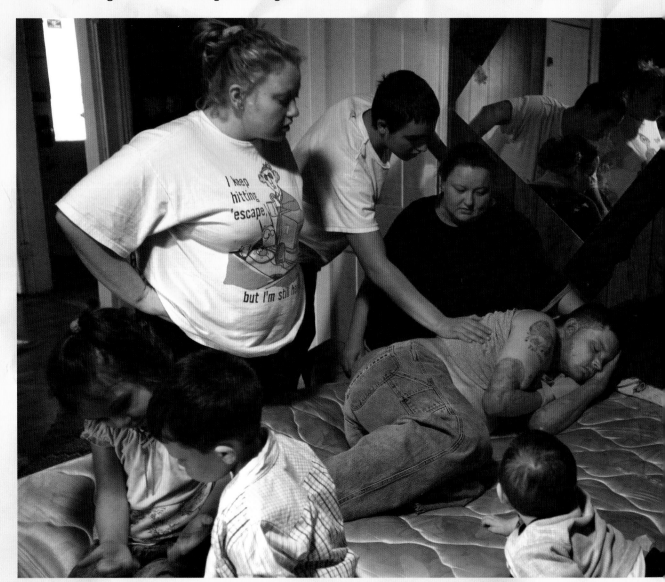

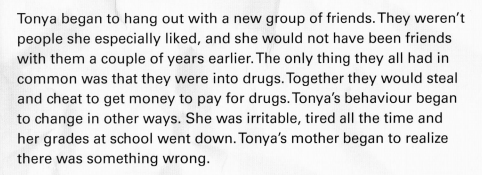

Interventions

An intervention happens when a group of family and friends band together because they are worried about someone. They meet to warn the person that they are concerned and want them to change their behaviour before it is too late. The families and friends of alcoholics and drug users use interventions to force them to get treatment for their addictions. Faced with so many people saying that they have a problem and need help with it, drug addicts find it hard to carry on claiming that they are really okay and can cope on their own.

stimulant, the user finds it hard to sleep. Tonya began to sniff heroin at the end of the day: heroin is a depressant, so it made it easier for her to get to sleep. Soon she had a taste for the relaxed feeling heroin gave and she started injecting it.

Tonya began to hang out with a new group of friends. They weren't people she especially liked, and she would not have been friends with them a couple of years earlier. The only thing they all had in common was that they were into drugs. Together they would steal and cheat to get money to pay for drugs. Tonya's behaviour began to change in other ways. She was irritable, tired all the time and her grades at school went down. Tonya's mother began to realize there was something wrong.

In the end Tonya's whole family realized she was ruining her life. Tonya's mother, aunts, uncle, older brother and two favourite cousins came to her house. One by one they each told her that they were worried about her and that they knew she was on drugs. At first Tonya denied it and tried to laugh it off. Her family wouldn't believe her, and in the end she broke down in tears and admitted that she was a heroin addict. Tonya promised to get treatment.

Today, Tonya has got her life back on track. She has finished high school, and is just about to start a college course. Best of all she is happy, healthy and free of drugs. 'I could never have saved myself without the help of my family, especially my mom,' she says.

◄ **This young man has been awake for several days while taking drugs. He has fallen asleep and cannot be woken up, so his family watch over him in case he needs medical attention.**

Tom's Story

Tom lives in Washington, DC. He first became addicted to drugs in his teens, and for ten years his drug addiction remained untreatable, despite many attempts at curing him. In fact his problems and behaviour got worse. Only when doctors discovered that Tom's drug use was hiding even deeper problems did he finally start making progress towards a cure.

Tom's mum first began to suspect there might be something wrong when his school grades began to drop. He had started hanging out with a new crowd of kids at school, and she thought maybe that was the reason. Then she overheard a phone conversation between Tom and one of his friends. It confirmed her worst fears – Tom was taking drugs. She and her husband confronted Tom, but he denied everything. Even so, Tom's parents forced him to go to a drug treatment centre.

Tom refused to take part in drugs therapy and wouldn't do anything the treatment centre suggested. His parents tried to force him by grounding him, but whenever they did this Tom would run away from home and go on a drugs binge. They told him he must not have drugs in the house and searched his room to make sure he was sticking to the rule. But nothing they did could get Tom off drugs.

▶ **This young man's father has discovered a cannabis cigarette in his room. Cannabis is a psychoactive drug. It affects the brain, changing the user's emotions.**

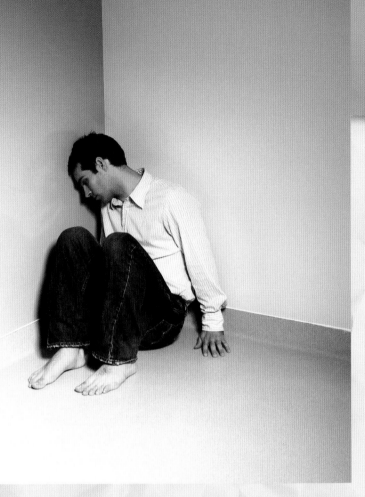

◀ Roughly one in ten cannabis smokers experience feelings of paranoia (that people are out to get them), confusion or worry. The effects of cannabis can last a long time, or be permanent. Young users are especially likely to develop long-term mental health problems.

Over the next few years Tom's problems grew steadily worse. He continued to live at home and also carried on taking drugs. Tom began stealing to pay for his habit. He regularly stole money from his parents. One day they were surprised to get a statement from their petrol charge card for thousands of dollars. They assumed it was a mistake, but then the truth came out: Tom had been offering to buy people petrol at a discounted price for cash, then paying for it using his parents' card. It was just one example among many of how Tom was willing to lie and cheat to get drugs.

As Tom's behaviour deteriorated, his parents began to wonder if there might be more to it than drug addiction. Then, on a family skiing trip, Tom had a psychotic episode. He talked gibberish and imagined things that were not there. The family came home early, and that night Tom tried to commit suicide. Tom was hospitalized, and doctors discovered that he was suffering from a mental illness – schizophrenia.

Schizophrenia

Schizophrenia is a mental illness that affects sufferers' senses. Among the most common symptoms are:

- hearing imagined voices, which seem to come from somewhere else

- believing that people are out to get you

- being unable to speak clearly or in an organized way

After being released from hospital, Tom was cared for by his mother. While he was dependent on her she was able to keep him away from drugs. But as Tom began to recover he started taking drugs again. This time Tom got hooked on crack cocaine. His mum remembers that 'the more he took, the more he wanted'. He had more psychotic episodes and was hospitalized on several occasions.

Tom's drug addiction and behaviour were starting to have a bad effect on his family. His mum and dad couldn't agree on how to deal with him and began to argue. His younger brother was also affected, having to listen to his parents shouting at each other and also getting less of their attention.

Tom's drug use had been partly an attempt to smooth out the emotional rollercoaster ride that was caused by his mental illness. Both drugs and mental illness make it harder for people to be sure of their true emotions and to share emotions with other humans. Tom's schizophrenia also made it much harder to persuade him to give up drugs. Although people he loved were telling him he needed to stop taking them, Tom was also hearing voices in his head that only drugs would block out.

Tom's problems were made worse by the difficulty he had in getting treatment. Mental health specialists were unable to treat his drug addiction. Drug counsellors did not understand his mental health problems. They found it puzzling that he rarely turned up to appointments, not knowing that voices in Tom's head were telling him not to attend.

Tom's recovery only started when the treatment for his schizophrenia began to work. His doctors found the right combination of prescription drugs to stop the voices in his head

Mental illness and drugs use

Long-term drug use is associated with several mental illnesses, including antisocial personality disorder, manic episodes and schizophrenia. According to the US National Institute of Mental Health, people suffering from these three illnesses are between 10 and 15 per cent more likely to develop drug addictions than non-sufferers. This may be because they are trying to use drugs to self-medicate — treat their mental illness themselves, without a doctor's help.

Source: www.usdoj.gov/ndic/pubs7/7343/index.htm

and put an end to his psychotic episodes. Finally, Tom was able to tackle his drug addiction. He began attending treatment regularly, and it has now been two years since he took any drugs that weren't prescribed by his doctors. It has been a long, hard road, but with a lot of help from his parents Tom seems to have freed himself from the twin troubles of mental illness and drug addiction.

◀ **Drug use often causes disagreements among families, as people argue about how to deal with the drug addict's problem. Sometimes this makes the addiction worse, as the addict uses drugs to escape from the tension.**

Delon's Story

As Delon's story shows, drug addicts often become expert liars. They are able to hide their addiction from the people closest to them, even their families, until finally their own bodies give them away. But Delon's story also demonstrates how even the most desperate addict can turn their life around.

As a teenager, Delon found it difficult to focus on his schoolwork or, later, his job. His parents remember that he always preferred to hang around with his friends than work. They hoped that as he grew up he would settle down. They had not guessed the truth about Delon's behaviour, which was that he had become addicted to heroin.

Delon's parents finally began to realize that he was lying to them. For instance, he claimed to have a job at a double-glazing company. But when they went to pick him up one evening, they discovered that he didn't actually work there. Next, money began to disappear from home. At first it was small amounts, then so much that it became impossible to ignore: Delon was stealing from his parents. Finally, they asked him to leave home.

Delon's parents saw less and less of him as he sank further into heroin addiction. Then one night he appeared at their door asking for money. His mother remembers, 'He looked like an old man of 70, not a young man in his mid-20s'. Delon collapsed and had to be taken to hospital. He had septicaemia – severe blood poisoning.

◀ **Many drug addicts live in terrible conditions, like this young man in La Paz, Bolivia. All their money is used to pay for drugs, and they have nothing left to spend on clothes, bedding and other things that would make their homes good places to be.**

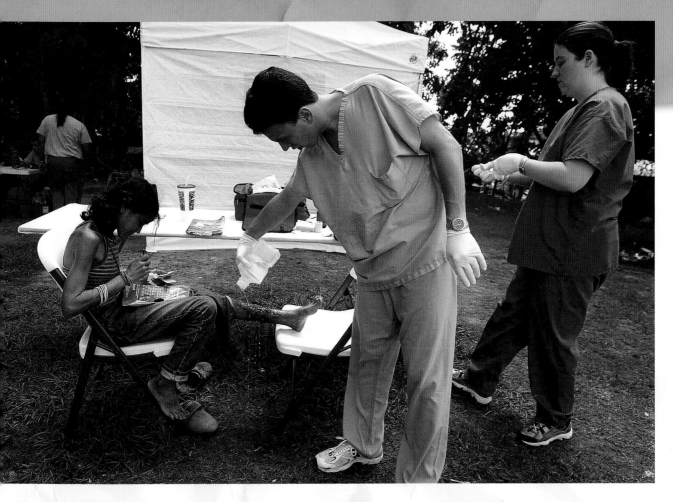

▲ **This drug addict in San Juan, Puerto Rico is injecting heroin at a 'safe-injection clinic'. The idea is that addicts get to use clean needles in a safe environment, which will help stop the spread of diseases such as hepatitis.**

Delon had come close to death. The experience forced him to accept the fact that drugs were killing him. He decided to fight his drug addiction – but there was one more test ahead. After leaving hospital, he was recognized on CCTV as a regular shoplifter. Delon was arrested and sent to prison. Even in prison he managed to stay clean, and after being released he began working for a drugs charity. Delon now spends his time helping other addicts to escape their dependence on drugs.

Drugs and prison

Drugs and prison form a vicious cycle for many drug addicts. To get money to pay for drugs, they break the law — shoplifting or committing burglaries. If caught, they are eventually sent to prison, where drug taking is commonplace. In fact, even people who go into prison clean sometimes come out with a drug addiction. Although many prisons offer addicts counselling or treatment, not all addicts are ready to accept this help. Instead, their time in jail reinforces their drug-taking habits, making it more likely that they will continue in their criminal ways when they get out.

Glossary

alcoholic A person who is addicted to alcohol.

Alcoholics Anonymous An organization that aims to help people cure their addiction to alcohol.

anaesthetic A substance that dulls pain.

bail A fee charged by the police or the courts before they will release someone suspected of committing a crime. If the suspect does not return when told, the person who pays the bail forfeits the money.

binge drink Drink large amounts of alcohol in a short space of time.

comedown The unpleasant after-effects of taking a drug.

crack cocaine A form of cocaine that can be smoked.

date rape Rape that happens when people have gone out on a date together or met in a social situation. Sometimes the rapist uses drugs to disable the victim.

decongestant A drug that stops or clears blocked-up or runny noses.

delirium tremens Withdrawal symptoms particularly associated with alcohol. They include visions of imaginary animals, fever, confusion and tremors.

dementia A deterioration or worsening of mental powers such as memory and organizational ability.

dope sick Withdrawal symptoms associated with a variety of drugs. They are similar to those of flu: aching limbs, shivering and a runny nose.

hardcore Particularly dedicated.

impotence An inability to achieve an erection, and therefore to have sex.

inhibitions Feelings that stop a person from acting in a particular way.

jack up A slang term for injecting drugs, particularly heroin.

joint A cigarette made completely or partly of cannabis.

legacy Long-term after-effects.

lethargy A feeling of tiredness and an inability to act.

manic Extremely or excessively active.

Narcotics Anonymous An organization that aims to help people cure their addiction to drugs.

overdose A dangerously large amount of a drug, causing hospitalization or death.

palpitations Unusually fast or irregular beating of the heart.

paranoid Unreasonably suspicious of other people and their thoughts or motives.

rehab Short for rehabilitation – a period or process during which someone is helped to return to good heath or normal life.

schizophrenia A mental illness that affects sufferers' senses, which may cause them to hear imagined voices inside their heads.

self-medicate Treating a medical complaint using drugs, without the help of a doctor.

septicaemia Blood poisoning. If left untreated it can cause death.

shoot up A slang term for injecting drugs.

skunk An especially strong form of cannabis, roughly three times as strong as normal cannabis.

street drugs Another term for illegal drugs – so-called because they are often sold on the street.

stroke A sudden blockage of blood flow in the brain, which can lead to loss of consciousness, loss of movement and/or slurred speech.

suicidal Wanting to kill oneself.

vaccine A substance given under medical supervision that triggers the body into building up resistance to a disease.

Further Information

Books

The Great Brain Robbery: What Everyone Should Know about Teenagers and Drugs by Tom
    Scott and Trevor Grice (Allen & Unwin, 2006)
Just the Facts: The Drugs Trade by Jim McGuigan (Heinemann Library, 2005)
Know the Facts: Drinking and Smoking by Paul Mason (Wayland, 2008)
Voices: Drugs on the Street by Anne Rooney (Evans Brothers, 2006)
What's That Got to Do with Me? Drugs by Antony Lishak (Franklin Watts, 2006)

Websites

checkyourself.com

This US-based site is aimed at teenagers who want to check out 'where they are with
drugs'. It includes video commentaries, stories from teenagers about their experiences
with drugs and quizzes to take about your own drug and alcohol consumption.

www.talktofrank.com

This excellent site has information about all kinds of different drugs, starting with an
A to Z of drugs, explaining how each one works, its effects and the problems that can
be caused by using it.

tinyurl.com/nt5hpz

This information page comes from the UK's National Health Service. It links to stories of
drug use, information about how drugs affect your body, places where you can get help
if you have a problem with drugs and much more.

tinyurl.com/6xmd6k

This page from the Australia Drug Information Network is a portal site, with links to
drugs advice organizations in all Australia's states and territories.

Index